separations

divorce

By Janine Amos

Photographs by Howard Davies

CHERRYTREE BOOKS

This book has been written to help children whose parents are about to split up or go through a divorce. It is also for friends of those children, to help them understand.

A CHERRYTREE BOOK

This edition first published in 2007 by Cherrytree Books, part of the Evans Publishing Group, 2A Portman Mansions, Chiltern St, London WIU 6NR

© Evans Brothers Limited 2007

Produced by

Nutshell
MEDIA
www.nutshellmedialtd.co.uk

Editor: Polly Goodman
Designer: D.R. Ink
Photography: Howard Davies
Based on the original edition of Divorce published in 1997.

With thanks to our models:
Joe, Mark, Cathy and Janet Chesson, Finley and Jane Walsh, Claire Pritchard, Hannah and Catherine Whitfield, Ella Cohen-Haddon, Frances Robinson, Martha and Beth Croydon, Ellen, Frances and Owen Bell-Davies, Maria Beckford, Fiona Curry and Jessica Halls. Special thanks to Lora Munro at Brighton Young Performers.

British Library Cataloguing in Publication Data
Amos, Janine
  Divorce. - Rev. ed. - (Separations)
  1. Divorce - Juvenile literature
  2. Divorce - Psychological aspects - Juvenile literature
  3. Children of divorced parents - Juvenile literature
  I. Title
  306.8'9

ISBN-13: 9781842344842

Printed in China.

Contents

Dear Gran,

Thank you for my birthday money. I'm buying a new game for my computer.

Last night Dad told me he was leaving. He doesn't like living here any more so he's going to live in a flat on his own. Dad says he'll see me at the weekends and I can stay at his place some school days too. The same thing happened to Jack, but his dad's always going away now and he doesn't see him much. He gives him kids' toys for his birthday like he doesn't know how old he is. I wish things could go back to how they were. Mum's crying all the time and shouting. It's horrible.

Are you coming to see us?

love Tom

Dear Tom,

I'm glad that you wrote to me. It's a hard time for you all, and you must be feeling very upset and confused.

Sometimes grown-ups can't get on any more. They stop loving each other but they don't stop loving you. Your mum and dad both love you very much, and both of them want to be with you. Remember that.

I'm sorry that your friend Jack doesn't see much of his father. That doesn't mean the same will happen to you. If your dad says he'll see you every week, then that's what he plans to do.

Your mum and dad are very hurt and sad at the moment, Tom. Keep talking to them. Tell them how you feel. You can always talk to me, either in a letter, an email, or on the telephone.

I'm thinking of you and I'm coming to see you soon.

With love,
Gran
xx

Christmas spirit

Bang! bang! bang! went Danny's foot against the kitchen chair. He knew it annoyed his mum. But today she pretended not to notice. Instead, she turned on the radio and a Christmas carol blared out. Danny hated the sound. And he hated the Christmassy smells coming from his mum's cooking. Danny hated most things since his dad had moved out.

Danny's mum handed him some knives and forks.

"Hurry up and set the table, Danny," she said. "Gran and Grandad will be here soon." Danny's mum smiled. But her eyes looked sad.

"It doesn't feel like Christmas without Dad," thought Danny. "Why is Mum pretending everything's the same?" Danny wanted to say this to his mum. But she only got upset when he talked about Dad.

Danny scowled. "You'll feel better when Gran and Grandad get here," said his mum gently.

"No, I won't!" shouted Danny. "It will be worse – much worse!"

Danny threw down the knives and forks and rushed out of the room.

Goldie, Danny's dog, followed him out to the back door. As Danny looked back, Goldie looked up at him with sad eyes and gave out a little whine.

"It's not that I don't want to see Gran and Grandad," Danny explained to Goldie. "But they always come for Christmas lunch. Doing everything the same will make me miss Dad more."

Just then the doorbell rang. "Let's go!" whispered Danny. He reached for Goldie's collar, opened the door and crept outside into the garden.

At the end of the garden, Danny sat down on a wall, hidden from view. It was cold, damp, and starting to get dark, but at least here Danny didn't have to pretend it was a happy Christmas.

Soon Danny's tummy rumbled. He felt in his pockets and pulled out some chocolate covered in fluff. It was left over from the bar his dad had given him last Saturday. Slowly Danny began to munch. He wondered if his dad was eating Christmas lunch all on his own. Two tears rolled down Danny's cheeks.

Soon Danny could hear his mum's footsteps coming along the path. Danny waited to be sent back into the house. Instead, his mum sat down next to him. She gave him a hug.

"Dad's never coming back home to live, is he?" whispered Danny, looking down at the ground.

"No," replied his mum quietly.

"Christmas makes it even harder," sighed Danny. "I wish we were a real family."

His mum thought for a while. "We are a real family, but we're a different sort of family now," she said at last, "and some things we do will be a bit different. Today you're having a Christmas Day with me, Gran and Grandad. Tomorrow you'll have a Christmas Day with your dad. What you must remember is that both Dad and I still love you. That is just the same."

Danny managed a wobbly smile. "We're having Christmas Day with Goldie, too," he said. "And he's ready for lunch!"

"How about ringing your dad first?" asked Danny's mum.

Danny nodded, and together they hurried back into the warm house.

Dear Sally

A lot's been going on around here. Mum and Dad had the biggest row and Dad moved out. They're getting a divorce.

I hate it. I can't tell anyone at school – not even Emma. Her Mum and Dad are always hugging each other, she won't understand. What was it like when your Dad went? I don't want to see my Dad ever again. He phones every day, but I won't talk to him.

Mum is snappy. She tells me off for being noisy. Then she tells me off for not talking to her.

School's OK. Our new teacher is Mrs. Roberts. She wears ugg boots and smiles a lot. She asked me if anything was bothering me and I said no.

Kate's having a sleepover next weekend. I don't think I'll go. I can't be bothered. Do you have sleepovers in America?

Mum says I can come and stay with you when I'm older, if we can save up.

Write soon

Love, Donna x

Dear Donna,

It was great to hear from you!

You sound angry and fed-up. That's just how I felt when my mom and dad split up. I wouldn't see my dad at first, either, but he kept coming over. At least talk to your dad on the phone, it will make you feel better. I bet he feels bad enough, without you ignoring him.

You say your mom snaps at you. Grown-ups are weird. They want to split up, then, when they do they still aren't happy. Maybe it takes them a while to get used to things. Maybe you should talk to your teacher about it. And tell your friends. My friends here were great. Life might be rotten right now — but it'll be worse if you stay at home feeling crummy.

Things are better for me now. Dad visits once a week and I stay at his place most weekends. We do crazy things together like go fishing or thread popcorn. My mom's got a boyfriend called Jasper!

Write soon

Love, Sally xx

ps Sure we have sleepovers in America! We invented them!

It's hard for everyone

When you first hear that your parents are splitting up, it's natural to have all kinds of strong feelings.

■ Danny feels sad that his family life is changing. He doesn't want his dad to live somewhere else. He wants things just as they used to be.

■ Danny also feels angry with his parents. They are grown-ups – they should keep him safe. At the same time he loves them both. He finds it hard to understand that they have stopped loving each other.

■ Like Danny, Donna feels angry that her dad has gone away. She's hurt too. She feels that he has left her.

■ Donna doesn't want to tell her friends at school that her dad has left. She feels different from her friends now. She's also worried about the future.

■ Children whose parents are divorcing are often moody and bad-tempered. Some find it hard to concentrate at school. They are often full of fears. They may feel that no one cares about them. They may be worried about the parent who has left home. Will they still see them?

■ When parents are worried and frightened themselves, it's sometimes difficult for them to give you their best attention. They might spend ages on the telephone to friends, talking things through. They might snap at you for no reason, or burst into tears. They might expect you to help out more at home.

■ If these changes seem hard or unfair, do tell someone. Talk to your mum or dad, or another adult you trust.

■ It's a difficult time for parents too. Some parents will be feeling like Tom's mum. She's sad that her marriage has ended. She's worried about the future too. At the moment she finds it hard to talk to Tom about his dad.

■ Tom's dad feels better now that he's left home. He couldn't stand any more rows. At the same time he's very sad not to be living with Tom every day.

■ Tom's parents have different ideas and feelings. But they agree on one thing. They love Tom and, wherever they are living, they will always be his mum and dad.

Helping yourself cope

If your parents are splitting up, you are bound to feel sad and confused. You may also feel hurt and angry. All these feelings are normal. You might even hate your mum and dad for what is happening, and that's OK, too. Sometimes, though, your feelings can be so strong that they are frightening.

These are some ways in which you can help yourself cope:

■ First of all, make sure you know what is going on. If there's anything practical you are not sure about – such as where you'll sleep at weekends or who will be taking you swimming – then ask.

■ Find someone to talk to about your feelings, fears and worries. If your mum and dad are too upset to listen properly, then say what you feel to a relative or teacher.

■ Remember that you are loved. Your parents are not divorcing you. And nothing you said or did caused their separation.

■ Remember, too, that you are not alone. There are other children in your school whose parents have split up, and who feel just like you.

■ You don't have to take sides. It's important to keep in touch with both your parents. If your mum or dad has left home, you can phone or write to them.

■ If you feel that visiting arrangements get in the way of something else you'd like to do, such as football practice or drama club, then do speak out. Perhaps a different arrangement would be possible.

■ Although you're sad, try to do the things you normally do. Keep up your hobbies and enjoy yourself with your friends.

Dear Gran,

Mum said you had a cold and that a letter would cheer you up.

I had a great half-term. I stayed four days with Dad and he took time off work. We painted my bedroom and put boats and ships on the wall. Dad did most of it but I helped. It's as good as my bedroom at home!

Dad's got a girlfriend. Her name's Linda. She came to tea but it felt funny because of Mum. She's not as pretty as Mum, she's got a big nose. I don't know why Dad likes her. He doesn't need a girlfriend, he can come back home if he's lonely.

I hope you feel better soon.

When are you coming to see us again?

Love, Tom

Dear Tom,

It was good to have a letter from you. My cold's almost gone now.

I'm glad that you and your dad enjoyed half-term. Your bedroom sounds super!

Try to be kind to Linda. If your dad likes her, I'm sure she's a nice person. Give her a chance and get to know her – you might make a new friend.

I know you'd really like your mum and dad to get together again. That isn't going to happen, Tom, and you can't do anything about it. They are making new lives for themselves – that means a new way of life for you.

We'll have another chat when I visit, if you like. I'm coming in two weeks – I can't wait!

Love, Gran

xx

Better or worse?

Even after your parents have separated for a while, you may still feel sad and confused.

■ Some children take a couple of years to settle into the new way of life. Other children worry because their parents seem to change a bit. They may start to wear different clothes or take up new hobbies. Keep talking to them. They are still the same people underneath.

■ In time, your parents will probably have a relationship with a new man or woman. At first Tom didn't like his dad's girlfriend. He felt a bit guilty about being with her. He worried that his mum would mind. He felt that Linda was a replacement for his mum, and this was painful for him.

■ Many parents decide to marry again or move in with someone new. At first you may feel sad or angry. You must finally give up any hope you had that your parents will get back together. Also, you may find it hard to share a parent when you have been used to having them all to yourself. You may feel jealous and pushed out. You may not like your parent's new partner.

■ It's normal to have all these feelings and it's all right to talk about them. If you don't want to tell your mum or dad, find a relative or a teacher who will listen.

Single-parent family

One or both of your parents may not have a new partner straight away. You may be part of what is called a single-parent family – like lots of other children. You can have fun with your friends and also do things with your parent. And your parent will make some new friends, too.

Give it a chance

Some children get on well with their mum and dad's new partner from the very beginning. For others, being part of this new 'stepfamily' may be more difficult. Sometimes there will be new half-brothers and sisters to get on with. It might help to remember these things:

■ Give everyone time. It takes a while to get to know new people. It may be two or three years before everyone in a stepfamily feels comfortable with each other. However long it takes is the right time for you.

■ No one is expecting you to love your new step-parent or stepfamily. Try to see them as friends. You can be friends with a step-parent and still love your real parent. It won't spoil your special feelings for each other.

■ Each family has its own rules. Your real mum may not mind you bouncing on the beds or eating in front of the TV – your stepmum may hate it. Talk about the rules for each home and stick to them.

■ Keep some time to be alone with each of your real parents. It's OK to ask for this.

■ The situation is new for everyone. People may make mistakes, so try to give everyone a chance.

■ If you have any fears or worries about your new family, talk about them. Problems don't go away if you keep them secret. If you can't talk to your mum or dad, tell a teacher or friend. Choose an adult you trust. If you can't think of anyone, ring one of the helplines on page 32.

Locked out

It was Friday afternoon. Kate and Gemma collected their coats and walked out of school. Gemma was going home. Kate was going to her dad's house.

Kate didn't say much. She kept her head down and dragged her feet. Gemma looked at her friend. "I thought you liked it at your dad's place?" she said.

"It used to be OK," replied Kate, sighing. "These days Miss Perfect's always there." Miss Perfect was Kate's dad's girlfriend. Her real name was Maria.

Gemma wrinkled her nose. She knew all about Maria's smart clothes, important job and fancy cooking. "Too good to be true," the girls had decided. They'd thought up the nickname together.

But there was something that Gemma didn't know. Miss Perfect and Kate's dad were getting married.

Kate waved goodbye to Gemma at the corner, and carried on alone. As she walked, Kate imagined Maria in a long wedding dress, smiling a perfect smile. "Now Mum and Dad will never get back together," thought Kate sadly. Her throat felt sore and she swallowed hard.

Slowly, Kate walked up to the front door and pressed the buzzer.

The door opened wide and Maria stood there. "Come in!" she said. She was dressed in black trousers and a shiny blouse.

"Where's Dad?" asked Kate, quickly. He always left work early on Fridays.

"He's still in a meeting," explained Maria. "He'll be a bit late today, I'm afraid." She gave Kate a bright smile.

Kate thought she would burst into tears. She turned away before Maria could see. She went back down the steps.

"Where are you going?" called Maria. "Come back!"

All at once, Kate felt angry. "You can't tell me what to do. You're not my mum!" she shouted.

Kate marched down the path and on to the pavement. She heard the door slam and Maria hurrying after her. "I've had just about enough," Maria panted, catching up. "I've rushed ..."

Suddenly Maria stopped. Kate turned round to look at her.

"We're locked out!" Maria groaned.

Kate waited to be told off. "Go on, put the blame on me," she told Maria silently. Instead, to Kate's surprise, Maria began to laugh. "What a perfect end to a rotten day!" she spluttered.

The sun had gone in and it was starting to get cold. Maria looked up and down the street. "What shall we do?" she asked, shivering. "Your dad won't be back for ages yet."

"We could go to a café," suggested Kate.

"I haven't any money on me," replied Maria.

"I have," answered Kate.

Inside the café, Kate and Maria sat with their mugs of tea. They stared out at the grey streets. At first, no one said anything. Kate thought how much younger Maria looked all of a sudden. She seemed much younger than her mum – but tired and cold. All at once, Kate felt sorry.

The man at the next table was eating a burger. Delicious smells drifted across to them. "I'm starving," Maria whispered, rolling her eyes. "I had to work through lunch."

Suddenly, Kate wanted to make everything all right. She rummaged through her school bag and counted up all her change. "I've got enough!" she said proudly. "I can buy you a burger, if you like."

"OK – half each," agreed Maria.

Munching her half of the burger, Kate watched Maria gobbling up her share. She didn't look at all perfect now. There was sauce on her cheek and she had to keep blowing her nose. But she still seemed happy. "My mum would have gone mad if I'd got her locked out in the rain," thought Kate.

"You've been really nice about all this," she told Maria after a while.

"It was an accident," said Maria. She looked hard at Kate. "I'm not trying to take your mum's place," she went on, carefully. "But I'd like to be your friend."

Kate went a bit red. "OK," she said. And she realised that it was.

Dear Sally

Things have really changed for me.
Remember I didn't see my dad for a while?
Well, in the end, we got talking on the phone.
Now I stay with him every two weeks, for a
weekend. He lives in an old house in the
country and he's got a dog called Jake. At
Easter we're going camping with Jake!

Mum and I get on really well, too. She's got a
part-time job, so sometimes I go to Emma's
house after school.

Mum picks me up after tea. Mum and I are
vegetarians now (like you!) Every week we
test out a new recipe. It's fun. How are your
family – and Jasper? (What a name!) Is he
nice?

Write soon

Love,

Donna x

Dear Donna,

Great to hear from you.

Guess what? Mom's getting married to Jasper. It's OK by me, he's a nice guy.

We had some trouble a while back. Jasper's kids came to stay for one week. They went in my room, they raided the refrigerator, they used my felt pens without checking. We had a big fight. Then we all got together and talked it through. Jasper made us do it — he's great like that. And it worked. I guess I found it hard not to be the only kid any more.

We're going camping too. Jasper's taking us to the mountains, looking for grizzlies.

Do you have bears in England?

Write soon

Love, Sally xx

Helplines

If you feel really alone, you could telephone or write to one of these offices, or look at their website. Sometimes the telephone lines are busy. If they are, don't give up. Try them again.

ChildLine
Freephone: 0800 1111
Website: www.childline.org.uk

National Stepfamily Association
Chapel House, 18 Hatton Place, London EC1N 8RU
Freephone: 0808 800 2222

NSPCC Child Protection Line
NSPCC headquarters, 42 Curtain Road,
London EC2A 3NH
Freephone: 0808 800 5000
Website: www.nspcc.org.uk